GENTLE HILLS

By

Marjorie Spalsbury

MARJORIE SPALSBURY'S POETRY BOARD OF DIRECTORS

Jeff R. Spalsbury
Lisa Estella Spalsbury
Sara Marjorie Spalsbury

Sandy L. Aldinger
Brian L. Buckles
Terre L. Buckles
Peyton N. Caudill
Seth M. Caudill

Dina A. Metzler
Alicia C. Schein
Ryan A. Poling
Aaron M. Schein

HONORARY MEMBERS OF THE BOARD

Barry A. Metzler
Stacie L. Metzler
Brady A. Metzler
J. Matt Schein
Diane de la Rosa Spalsbury
Mary Beth Buckles

FORWARD

Gentle Hills is the collected poems of
Marjorie Spalsbury. The rolling, gentle hills
surrounding her hometown of Logan, Ohio
were always loved by our mother. The
beautiful Hocking County valley, its people,
trees, flowers, birds and animals were a
constant source of inspiration and joy for
her. Deeply religious, she had a very
personal rapport with God and a strong
belief in the goodness of all God's children.

When she died in April 2007, she left a
legacy of love, laughter and joy that was
instilled in all who knew and loved her. Her
granddaughter, Lisa Spalsbury wrote about
her memories of her grandmother while
spending summer vacations in Logan: "I
think of polka dots, keys in every size, the
stationary bicycle in the kitchen, grilled
cheese sandwiches (I'll only have one
nibble, she would say with a twinkle), her
funny giggle, her 20 minute catnaps (I'm
just checking my eyelids for leaks), her
beautiful garden, her love of books, walking
down Main Street for our back to school
outfits, shakes at the Shake Shoppe, walks

back and forth to the pool, catching
lightning bugs, hugs when it was thundering
(it's only the angels bowling, she'd say),
sitting out on the porch watching the rain,
the wet cold towels she'd bring in and put on
our heads when it was soooo hot at night,
her fantastic love of all of us and her great,
bright smile!!"

You, also, will sense her great, bright smile
in all her poems as she shared her love of
life, of the Hocking Valley she so loved, of
people and the children she cared so much
about, and of an unbending faith in God. As
you read these poems you will hear our
mother's sweet, gentle voice and if they
make you smile, then know that she will be
pleased. I'm sure God's angels will pass on
your joy of her poems to her.

Jeff R. Spalsbury

Website: www.JeffRSpalsbury.com

DEDICATION
To my family, who have
given me so much love
and encouragement.

CONTENTS

GENTLE HILLS

I was born in this land of gentle hills,

Forest glad, verdant green,

White with snow in winter,

White with dogwood blossoms in the spring.

This land of the Hocking is so filled

With beauty

A lifetime isn't long enough to see

All of my gentle hills under the changing sky

But I shall try, I shall try!

WINTER, SPRING, SUMMER, FALL

PRAYER FOR WINTER DAYS

O, God,

Help me to make winter days

Seem warm and bright.

When icy winds blow

Make me so glow

With good cheer

We won't miss the summer sun.

When the day is done

May our supper table be as gay

As a picnic on a June day.

And when the cold dark falls

May the love between us

Be like a golden light

To warm our hearts

Thru out the night.

WINTER IN OHIO

The winter cold overnight

Have turned my garden frosty white.

It glistens like a thousand fiery diamonds

In the sun.

There'll be many stormy gales

Before this winter's done.

In the flickering light of the fire's glow

I'll listen to the north wind blow

It's winter in Ohio.

TREE IN WINTER

Your leaves are brown and withered now

Your branches charcoal against the winter sky

Yet in your lofty majesty, how beautiful you are

As you stand serene, while winter winds fly by.

FIRST SNOW

"It's snowing, it's snowing," the children cry

As from the dark and leaden sky

The soft white flakes come fluttering down.

And I, with dust cloth and broom in hand,

Watch my world become a fairyland

And I am a child once more.

WINTER NIGHT

On this quiet winter night

In my silent world of white

The gnarled pine tree stands

Dark against the sky.

There're snow prints of tiny animals

Scurrying home, well fed

And in a sheltered crevice of the garden wall

A small, blue violet proudly lifts its head.

PRAYER ABOUT WINTER BIRDS

Dear God,

Thank you for the winter birds.

I'm glad You had some stay

To share the cold days

With me.

They wait each morning

In the old pine tree

For the food I bring.

And afterwards

The snow is covered

With the feathery little tracks

They make.

What a joy to hear their songs

Even when icy winds are blowing.

If they can sing

In February

So can I, God.

Thank you again

For the winter birds.

WINTER GARDEN

My winter garden is frosty white

It glistens like a thousand

Fairy diamonds in the sun.

Each twig and branch has become

An intricate design.

I hear the wind blow

Thru the apple tree

It makes a tinkling sound

Come with me

And see my

Winter-bound garden

White with snow.

WINTER'S SONG

Sing a song of winter

Of snowflakes blowing wild and free

Of small bright birds that come

To the feeder in the apple tree.

Sing a song of winter

Of cold dark nights

When everything is still.

God bless us all

And this old house,

Sleeping on the hill.

WINTER BIRDS

I heard the winter birds

Sing this morning

In a world that seemed

Dark and gray and grim.

So I, too,

When my day

Is dark and gray and grim

Shall count God's blessings

And sing my song for Him.

SEED CATALOGUES

Seed catalogues can turn winter to spring.

When the ground is covered with snow

And the wild north winds blow

The catalogues come and make my gardener's heart sing

Of blossoming apple trees and birds on the wing

Of violets and white hyacinth

Yellow forsythia and mint

The sweet smelling earth and all green growing things.

PRAYER ON A WINTER DAY

Heavenly Father,

My garden lies asleep.

Under the ice and snow

And a cold wind blows

Thru the bare branches

Of the apple tree.

Sometimes in the winter

I feel just like my garden.

I too, am asleep

Under the ice and snow.

Please help me

Keep spring in my heart.

When days are dark and dreary.

Help me to be as bright

As the summer's sun.

Let my laughter be as gay

As children playing

Under a warm blue sky.

May the fire of love

Burn brightly in my heart

And warm all those I love.

WINTER'S SKY

There's something about a blue winter sky

That fills my heart with delight.

In a world of only charcoal hues

How I love this bright blue!

So, blow, winter wind, blow

Snow, winter cold, snow

I will treasure this azure sky

On each long, winter night.

A SPRING DAY IN WINTER

I love an unexpected

Spring-warm day

In the middle of the winter.

It's as if God says

I'm still here

Amid the cold and snow and ice.

Never fear,

My little ones.

Summer's on its way

With its skies of blue.

So enjoy this special day

That I made

Just for you.

REDBIRD

On a cold dark February morning

I heard a redbird sing.

His song filled my day with sunshine

And gave me a promise of spring.

WILL SPRING NEVER COME?

This has been such

A long, cold winter

I thought spring would

Never come.

But what do you know!

We just saw the

First robin

Singing in the snow.

THOUGHTS OF SPRING

I lie in bed,

On winter nights

Thinking sweet thoughts

Of spring.

I can almost see

The grass grow.

I can almost hear

The robin sing.

While snow and icy winds

Batter at my window so

I can almost smell

The lilacs

I can almost see

The firefly's glow.

ANTICIPATION

There's the soft drip, dripping

Of melting snow today.

I know, beyond a doubt,

Spring is on the way.

Though it's still cold

And the trees are bare

There was, for just a second,

The scent of lilacs in the air.

FIRST SPRING FLOWER

There's a bright splash of color

Under the dogwood tree

The first blue crocus is blooming

A gift from March to me.

BIRDS

The grosbeaks are back

My bird feeder is alive with color

Such flashing of gold and white and black.

Once more I marvel at such beauty

And God, who set the moon and stars in space

Yet made these small bright birds for me.

THE SMELL OF APRIL

There is an indescribable fragrance

In the air this morning.

Try as hard as I might

I can't say

It is this or that.

Perhaps it's just spring aborning.

Maybe it's the sun-warmed earth,

Newly turned,

And violets and crocus and new baby leaves

And the first soft breeze

From the south

So full of the promise of summer

You want to clutch it

To your heart

And never let it go.

It's all these things

Stirred together by a winter's wind

That's lost its chill

That make up this wonderful smell

Called April.

SNOW IN APRIL

Just because the crocus

And violets and forsythia are blooming

Is no reason you should be assuming

That spring is here to stay.

Now, the icy winds are blowing

And it is snowy white.

Winter must have his last fling.

But have patience.

Perhaps, this very night

With gentle steps

She'll come, singing.

And winter will concede defeat

And leave the earth

To spring.

SPRING RAIN

Spring rain is a gentle thing.

Summer rain is stormy

Fall rain's cold and sad

But spring rain is a singing thing

That awakens

All God's creations.

SPRING'S ASSISTANT

I hurry thru each task

Then rush outside to see

If there's another flower in bloom

Or more leaves on the tree.

I just can't bear for spring

To add a single new thing

Without me.

THERAPY

We all have troubles

How well I know that's true.

Yet when I dig

In the sweet, sun-warmed earth

Troubles fly away.

And like the trees turning green

And the nesting birds

And each new blade of grass,

I, too, am part of God's creation

And I'm glad I'm alive.

SUMMER BREEZE

A breeze, fragrant with the scent of flowers

Rustles the leaves of the maple trees

And cools me like a gentle fan.

All stress and strain fade away

And I feel like God has touched me

With His healing hand.

APRIL SUNDAY

I walk to church today

On this bright April morning

In a quietly sedate way

As befits a grandmother.

But inside I skip and sing

About the sights and smells of spring

And God and I both smile with glee

At the joy felt by the other me.

SPRING CLEANING

In the spring, my grandmother cleaned

Her house from nook to cranny.

Swept and scrubbed and polished

'Til it shone like a new copper penny.

This spring I'd like to clean

The world from nook to farthest cranny

Sweep and scrub and polish

'Til it, too, shines like a new copper penny.

SOUNDS OF SPRING IN A SMALL TOWN

I hear them all,

The sweet sounds of spring

In my small town.

The whirl of the children's roller skates,

The crunch of my neighbor's garden rake

The rolling thunder in the hills,

The song of a redbird on my window sill

The gentle rain at night

The wind that blows the boy's kite

And if I listen very, very carefully

I can even hear the trees

Unfold their new, green leaves.

APRIL RAIN

Softly it falls on my windowpane

This gentle, sweet April rain

And I wash the breakfast dishes

And sing

Wake up, my world,

It's spring, it's spring!

I SHOULD CLEAN THE HOUSE TODAY

I should clean the house today

But spring has come

And my violets are blooming

So here I sit in the sun,

Unrepentant.

PRAYER ON A SPRING MORNING

God,

Your world is so beautiful

This dewy, spring morning

Washed clean by the rain last night.

Please, wash all of us, too,

This dewy, spring morning

Make us new and clean and bright.

SPRING SONGS

The alarm clock rings

Yet here I lie

Listening to the birds sing.

Nestled in the lilac tree

They're singing songs of love

It's my early morning symphony.

THANKFULNESS FOR A SPRING MORNING

Dear God,

Everywhere I look

I see your hand at work

Creating beautiful things

For me to see.

The new leaves on our maple tree

And the myriad of flowers

That fill my yard

Thank you for all these

And for the busy garden bee

That cheerfully goes about his task

Dear God,

This one thing I ask

As I watch my days unfurl

Never let me lose

This sense of wonder and delight

In your world.

SUMMER DAYS

I love the sunshine of summer

The bright, golden shimmering light.

Yet, I also love the hours of rain

Soft and cool, as a silver haze

My beautiful kaleidoscope of summer days.

IRONING ON A SUMMER DAY

I'm ironing on a hot summer day

But my mind is far away

On my secret island

Where the spicy trade winds blow.

After that, I'm in the mountains

In the midst of cool, soft falling snow.

Then I talk to God of this and that

And after our little chat

I'm so amazed to see

The bottom of my ironing basket

Looking up at me.

DANDELIONS

Children love the yellow dandelions

And pick them for their bouquets.

Most grown-ups dig them up

And throw them all away.

But there is a secret

Only angels know

God made them just for children

That's why the dandelion grows.

AFTER THE RAIN

Everything is so green,

Like all the St. Patrick Days

You've ever seen!

Each blade of grass and leaf

Sparkles and shines

Reflecting the sun's glow

And all this is mine!

WILD ROSE

Deep in the woods, I saw

A wild rose entwined in a tree.

No one was there to see its gentle beauty.

Only God and me.

OCTOBER THOUGHTS

The leaves on my maple tree

are turning gold.

There is a feeling in the air

that tells me

soon it will be cold

and my world will become crystal white.

So it's pleasant just to sit

on the back steps and sip

a cup of tea

under an October sun

that's still warm and bright

and listen to the redbird sing

while I dream of all the flowers I'll grow

next spring.

APPLE TREES

My great, great, great grandmother

Came to Ohio

Following a wagon's track,

With the roots of her apple trees

Tied on the back.

When I planted my apple trees

It gave me such pride,

Tho worlds separate us,

She stood by my side

FALL LEAVES

The leaves on the dogwood tree

Are turning red.

They fall, like gentle rain,

Upon my head.

I can't complain

That winter's on its way,

I am surrounded

By too much beauty today.

MAPLE TREES

In the spring

My maple trees

Like two prim and proper ladies

Unfurl above their heads

A leafy parasol.

But in the fall

They become two gypsy girls

Clad in gold and red

Flirting with the sun,

Dancing with the autumn wind

Until the winter comes.

RAKING LEAVES

I rake the leaves

Into a fragrant pile

Of scarlet, gold and red.

A small child runs and jumps

In gay abandon,

Leaves clinging to hands, feet and head.

I stand and watch with gentle joy,

Quiet as a mouse.

Thank you, God, for autumn leaves

And small children

Playing around my house.

WEATHER REPORT

It looks like snow

The old ones say

And I smile to myself

How can they know—

And yet—

After I sweep and dust and bake

I glance out the window

And see the first snowflake.

A GOLD CAT...ALBERT

STRAY KITTEN

He came to us one snowy night,

A cold, wet ball of fur,

That gave my heart a boost.

He stayed with us

Fat, sleek and gold.

Now, he's the ruler of the roost.

CAT IN MY GARDEN

He comes on velvet steps

To watch me,

A golden cat, with amber eyes,

All curiosity.

Sitting by my side,

He surveys his domain,

With silent pride.

Then while I dig,

Here on my knees,

He's off to chase

A bumblebee.

CAT

He's elegantly gold with tawny eyes

When the weather's hot, he sleeps

Under the lilac bush.

Does he dream of chasing butterflies

And bees

Or

Does he dream of a time, eons past

When he sat on a Pharaoh's knee

And they ruled the world together?

NEFERTITI AND ME

NEFERTITI

When I first saw the statue

Of ancient Egypt's beautiful queen

I knew we'd met before.

It was like a dim, half-forgotten,

Half-remembered memory

Being repeated once more.

It was like stepping thru

A strange, yet oddly familiar door.

But how could a queen

Of the eighteenth dynasty

And a woman in a small town

In Ohio

Have ever met?

And yet … and yet …

CHILDREN AND GRANDCHILDREN

ON CHILDREN GROWING UP

When your children are growing up

Such dreams you dream for them,

As you bandage cuts and scrapes

And lengthen pants and hems.

As they grow up, you grow up, too.

Your schemes are not so wild.

To be a good man or woman

Is the wise dream for your child.

GROWN UP CHILDREN

My children are all grown

With families of their own

Yet to me

They're still just three.

COMING HOME FOR A VISIT

The children are coming home for a visit!

The old house is in a whirl of activity

The likes of which you've never seen.

Such scrubbing and dusting and polishing,

Such washing and ironing and baking,

Such weeding, grass cutting, bedmaking.

Now everything's ready, the porch light is lit,

We all breathe a sigh of contentment.

The children are coming home for a visit!

GRANDCHILDREN

It should come as no surprise

That I look at you with grandmother eyes

Your faults are infinitesimally small

Your virtues, great beyond recall.

It's plain to tell, as you can see

You're practically perfect,

At least to me.

TERESA*

She's a dark ponytail

Ballet slippers and books.

She's bright colors and music

Hair ribbons and sun kissed looks.

THE UNICORN*

I walked through the woods

One day in spring

The wind was soft and fragrant

With the promised flowers

That April brings.

I had looked in vain

So many years before.

Only once when I was small

Did I see him, standing tall

In the meadow by the pine tree.

Suddenly, I could hear my heart sing

As if I had been reborn.

For there before me now

Eating the small white violets

Was my unicorn.

For one brief moment

The world stood still

And there was only

My unicorn and me

On a wind-swept hill.

* For Terre L. Buckles

BRIAN*

He's blond tousled hair

Bicycle, games and football

He's scary stories at bedtime

Puffed wheat and cookies, and a boy

growing tall.

*For Brian L. Buckles

ALICIA*

She's eyes like the summer sky

Raggedy Ann, books and blocks

She's a giggly wee pixie

The summer sun and a sandbox.

*For Alicia C. Schein

LISA*

She's laughing dark eyes

Hair shiny as a robin's wing

She's dancing feet and tea parties

Dolls and songs to sing.

FOUR YEARS OLD*

Now that Lisa is four

She's decided she's

A baby no more

There are worlds to explore,

People to see

Now that she's quite grown up

And no longer three.

*For Lisa E. Spalsbury

TO AN UNBORN GRANDCHILD*

Dear little child, in your soft warm nest

Who knows but on some bright April morn

The whole world may be in a better place

Just because you've been born.

SARA*

Sara's sweet and very dear

A joy to all the family.

Admirers come from far and near

They simply will not let her be

For she was made to love and hold.

Today, our Sara's one week old.

For Sara Marjorie Spalsbury

THOUGHTS AT THE AIRPORT

I watched you walk away

I didn't cry

Although I wept inside.

I waved and smiled.

It is so hard to say goodbye

Even to a grown up child.

DIVIDENDS

Grown up children can bring you joy

Beyond your fondest dreams

They also give you grandchildren

That's icing for the cake, it seems

TO A FARAWAY CHILD

It's a gloomy dark winter day

But I know something

That would make it seem

Like the first day of May.

The sight of your dear face

And this place would gleam

Like the summer sun.

Since that can't be

I'll just close my eyes

And here you are

Once more with me.

MY GRANDMOTHER'S HEART

My grandmother's heart is elastic

For it can stretch and grow

And without a bit of strain or fuss

Create a very special spot

For each new grandchild born to us.

LEGACY

I wish

That all my life

From the moment of my birth,

I had lived with only

The sweet and gentle things of the earth.

But since that cannot be,

Oh, my children,

Listen to me!

Some money I shall leave you

But this is my real legacy.

Don't let a day go by,

Without treasuring the beauty

Of the earth or sea or sky.

Love and protect the sweet and gentle things.

Note them all,

The big and small.

Those special moments

When your heart sings.

Teach this to your children

That they may teach their children, too.

For you see, my dears,

My legacy to this sad, old world

Is you.

FIRST DAY AT SCHOOL*

Her hair is brushed

Until it gleams.

Two barrettes hold back the sides

Like shiny wings.

She stands still

While I inspect her dress,

Newly starched, carefully pressed.

Her socks are turned down

At the proper places.

Her shoes are polished

With new shoelaces.

I hold her hand

Until we reach the door

We turn and smile at each other

Once more

And say goodbye.

Little one, goodbye.

It's time for you to spread your wings.

It's time for you to fly.

*For Alicia C. Schein

GOALS

When I was young

I had so many goals.

But now that I am getting old

I find that goals are hard to reach.

Dear Lord,

If I can have but one,

Let it be to teach

My children to find their way to you.

To live good lives

And to themselves be true.

Oh, Lord,

When all is said and done

Let this goal be the one.

TEA PARTY

TEA PARTY

When I was very young

My grandmother served me tea

In delicate, hand-painted cups.

We talked of this and that

And I felt so very grown-up.

Today, a gracious old lady

Served me tea and petits fours,

Called me a dear child,

And I, with grown-up children of my own,

Felt so very young, once more.

GRANDPA

GRANDPA

He never came to visit us

Without a sack of peppermint candy

In his pocket.

This warm, gentle man.

Tho' years have passed,

The smell of peppermint, to this day,

Fills me with sweet memories

Of grandpa and a small girl, holding hands.

GRANDFATHER

My grandfather was

A warm, loving man

Who lived life to the brim.

Oh, God,

Let me grow old

Just like him.

THE JOY OF GIVING

I grew up with a wonderfully

Generous grandfather

And some of that rubbed

Off on me.

When I was young I thought

Glory be

The joy is in the getting.

But the joy is in the giving

It can turn a gloomy week bright

It can warm your heart

On a cold frosty night.

If you don't believe me

Try it some dark day

And see.

GETTING OLDER

PRAYER ON GROWING OLD

God, help me grow old gracefully

In my small world and after

Leave my children a legacy

Of joy and love and laughter.

YESTERDAY

I know it was only yesterday

That I was young

And carefree and gay.

In all of my daydreams

The whole world was mine.

I held the sunbeams

In the palm of my hand.

I built golden castles

On the wet sand.

I rode a white pony

With silvery wings.

I knew all the songs

The cricket sings.

I danced and I laughed

In the wind and rain.

Never again will the world

Be the same.

I was dewy and fresh

As the first day in May.

I know it was only yesterday.

THE MIDDLE YEARS

Swiftly, the years fly by

And we are middle aged.

Yet this is no time to sigh

That the best of life is gone.

The middle years are part of God's plan

With a wisdom and beauty

All their own

So come, my love, and hold my hand

We still have dreams to dream.

THE FALL OF MY LIFE

I am in the fall

Of my life.

The years swirl around me

Like the leaves of the multicolored

Trees of autumn.

Brown and gold

Yellow and red.

So are the days I hold

In the hollow of my hand.

Part sunshine

Part rain and cold.

Yet together they form the design

God meant for me.

I thank Him for all the blessings

He has sent.

I love my fall time life

I am content.

REGRETS

Why didn't someone tell me

When I was very young

That I'd have such regrets

For the things I haven't done.

For poems I haven't written

For songs I haven't sung

For books I haven't read

For flowers I haven't planted

For kind words I haven't said

The years fly by so swiftly

And in looking back

Was I a good mother

To my children?

As a wife,

What did I lack?

Did I appreciate all the beauty

That there was to see?

Then God

In a still, small voice

Quietly answered me

You'll have time to fulfill your dreams

Thru all eternity.

LOVE

LOVE

Love is a funny thing.

When you're in the spring

Of your life

You think you know it all.

But now I'm in the fall

Of my life

And this I know,

Love grows and grows.

What a beautiful thing it will be

In the winter snows

Of my life.

OLD AND NEW

I love so many old things…

Sweet little old ladies

Gallant old men

Old houses and trees

Handwoven coverlets

Pewter pitchers, old keys.

I love so many new things…

New mothers that sing.

Sleepy-eyed little babies

First buds of spring

Soft kittens and mittens

All bright shiny things.

ON SAYING GOODBYE

It's hard to say goodbye

When skies are

Leaden gray.

So,

If you must,

Say good bye

When skies are blue above,

Or else,

Be so full of love

For that dear face

You think not of the sadness

Of this time in space

But of that joyous day

When once more you say,

Hello.

THINK OF ME

Think of me

Once in a while,

With love.

And I will feel it

Across the miles

That separate us.

And for a brief moment

We will be together again.

And the distance between us

Will disappear

And the time we're apart,

Be less.

Your thoughts

Like a tender touch,

Will heal my loneliness.

LOVE: YOUNG AND MIDDLE AGED

When you're young, love is

A gay, wild, happy thing,

Fiercely burning,

Tragic and funny.

When you're middle aged, love is

A gentle, tender, caring thing

Brightly burning,

Sweet as honey.

LOVE SONG IN THE NIGHT

I will sing a love song

To you this night

With words so sweet and bright

You'll think of

Blossoms in the spring

Walks in the rain

And summer birds that sing

Outside our window, soft and low

Come and sing along with me.

Dear one, I love you so.

I THINK OF YOU

In the night

When the stars

Hang silent in the sky

I think of you

And smile.

In the day

While I go about my work

I think of you

And rejoice.

Winter, summer

Spring and fall

It matters not at all

What time it is.

I think of you

And my thoughts

Soar like a kite.

I am so glad

You are in my life.

LOVE LIES

Tell me I'm beautiful

Gorgeous, witty and wise.

I know it isn't really true

But I love those sweet love lies.

HELD TOGETHER BY LOVE

The world is held together by love

Make no mistake about it

Man for woman

Woman for man

For a child from father and mother

Without this heavenly glue that binds us

We'd be lost in outer space

Aliens to each other.

It forms a circle of hands

That reaches around the world and back

And over it all

God's love for us

Is the final act.

CHRISTMAS

THE FIRST CHRISTMAS

Tell me, Jesus,

On the night you were born

Did the animals really talk?

Did the straw in your manger bed

Really glow as if it was made of gold?

Did the little lame shepherd boy really walk?

And did the innkeeper's still-born baby

Come to life, as I've been told?

Did the small black sheep really turn white

On that wonderful night so long ago?

And did the doves in the stable

Sing you a lullaby so sweet and low

Even the angels rejoiced?

I wish I could have been there

To see all these wonderful sights.

But most of all

I wish I could have seen you

On that first Christmas night.

I LOVE EVERYTHING ABOUT CHRISTMAS

I love everything about Christmas

From Jesus' birth to red candles and holly.

The songs we sing, the brightly lit stores

Neighbors greeting neighbors

Crisp cold weather, ornaments on green pine

I love the look and feel and smell of it!

Cookies and nut bread, candy canes and ribbons

Gifts under the tree, the Christmas angels

Children's eyes all bright with wonder

And bells that ring out at midnight saying

Jesus is born, Jesus is born, Jesus is born!

CHRISTMAS TREES

Christmas trees are wondrous things.

They fill the house with the sweet smell of pine

Covered with ornaments, they twinkle and shine

Like the children's eyes.

They bring a magic something to the house

A feeling of peace on earth and joy

Funny how the Christmas trees

Makes me think of

Bethlehem and Mary's baby boy.

CHRISTMAS REUNION

God,

I'll have to confess

I'm most impressed

With all the strings

You had to pull

To make this reunion possible.

But here we are

Together again

After so many years.

I look at them all

The big and the small

Thru happy tears.

My heart is so full of love

I lift

This grateful prayer to you.

Oh, God,

Thank you for this wonderful gift.

CHRISTMAS EVE — LATE

It's Christmas eve, at last.

The children are finally fast

asleep and I look around the house.

The presents are under the tree.

The turkey is ready to bake.

The pies, all three,

are cooling on the shelf.

Tomorrow will be a busy day

I should go to bed myself

But here I stand instead

So full of love and joy

Thank you, dear God, thank you

For your newborn baby boy.

CHRISTMAS

Hear the angels' song

Ringing sweet and clear

Telling all the world

Jesus Christ is here.

See His star

In the dark and frosty sky

Shining with such heavenly light

It almost makes you cry.

Truly

Love has come to earth

This night.

FOR EVERYTHING COMES FROM GOD ALONE*

3 A.M.

It's 3 a.m. and I can't sleep

So I think of many things

Instead of counting sheep—

Of children near and far away

And what I plan to do today,

My husband sleeping here by me,

The wind singing in the maple tree,

Of God and his love so deep,

Then, quieted, I go to sleep.

*Romans 11:36

THE ANSWER

I'd shout it from the hills

Print it in every newspaper

Put it on television and radio, too.

I'd cry out to the whole world

Let's do God's will if only for a day.

What a beautiful day that would be!

SONGS OF JOY

Let those who will

Sing songs of grief.

I'll sing songs of joy

And tap my feet.

Even when the days are dark

Oh, God, let me hear the lark

That sings

And bring those I love

Eternal spring.

TOGETHER WE CAN

I had something to do.

"It's impossible," I cried.

But God said, "Hold My Hand.

And what you couldn't do alone,

Together, we can."

WHEN I MEET GOD

When I meet God face to face

I vow

I don't want to be a stranger to Him,

So I'm cultivating His acquaintance

Now.

HEALING HANDS

Dear God,

As I rock my sick child

This dark night,

Help her

And all the other little ones

Racked with pain.

Place your cool, healing hand

On each small fevered brow

And heal them.

And thank you so much

For caring.

THE JOY ROAD

Jesus said,

"Come, follow me.

Let me show you the way

you should go."

I said,

"Not today, Lord.

I want to dance and play

with my friends."

But when it got dark

my friends ran away

and I was left alone and afraid.

There He was again.

And I said,

"Yes, Lord

This time I'll come."

And turned with solemn face

and sober step to follow.

He said, with a smile,

"Did you think you

wouldn't dance and sing

along My way, dear child?"

So I gave Him my load

of cares

and no longer afraid and alone.

We have danced and sung

down the joy road

toward home.

PRAYER FOR THOSE WITH NO BREAD

Dear God,

I baked bread today

And as I pulled the loaves

All brown and fragrant

From the oven

I remember all the mothers

Who have no bread

To give their children.

Please,

In your infinite mercy

Help those who have no food

May I do my part, too

So that between us all

No one will go to bed hungry this night.

PRAYER FOR INNER LIGHT

Dear God,

As blind Bartimaeus called out

To our Lord

As he passed by

So, I, too, call out

Jesus, Son of David,

Have mercy upon me.

Help me to see

Not only with my eyes

But with my heart and mind as well.

Don't let me be blind

To the needs of this troubled world.

From those in high places

To the youngest child

In the family

May I be mindful of them all

In my daily prayers.

Amen.

PRAYER FOR LOST CHILDREN

Oh, God,

Comfort all your lost children this night.

All the lost, lonely, tired ones

The hurt, mixed up, mired ones

Fill our hearts with thy light.

PRAYER FOR A SATURDAY MORNING

God,

Maker of heaven and earth

Maker of soft, cool breezes

Sunshine and shadows

Hollyhocks and ladybugs

Thank you for this beautiful

Saturday morning.

SKY AT NIGHT

When I stand under the sky at night

I feel I could reach out in space

And touch God's face.

JUSTICE

It isn't fair the hurt ones cry

And this I really can't deny.

For they are right

But where's it written

This old world is fair

Or that you'll always

Get your share

Of the world's delights?

Yet this I know

We're not alone.

God waits to guide those

Far from home

Thru the starless night.

I GRIEVED FOR SO MANY THINGS

I grieved for so many things,

Children treated cruelly,

Old people with no one to really care,

All the hurt ones in war and famine and floods.

I cried to heaven,

"What can I do to help?

This sadness is so hard to bear."

And God, gently replied,

"I have people who need you

Right where you are.

Start there."

EVERYDAY THINGS

The foolish man takes for granted

All the lovely, little everyday things

Accepting them as his due.

The wise man knows they belong

In the center of life

To be treasured each day

Like small, rare jewels.

HEAVENLY FATHER

Heavenly Father,

I've grumbled all day

To myself and you

About the bitter weather

And yet this morning

I saw a redbird

In the big pine tree

That was so beautiful

I rejoiced at the sight.

I got a cheerful letter

From a friend

Who's been very sorrowful.

I talked to my son and then my daughter

In their faraway homes

And our laughter rang

Across the miles.

Forgive my grumbling.

Help me to be aware

Each day of all your blessings

Amen.

EARLY MORNING

I love the early morning.

That dewy fresh

Sweet smelling time

When the world seems new.

And some day

I wouldn't be a bit surprised

To see God there

Enjoying the early morning, too.

DARK THOUGHTS

Dark thoughts come unbidden

And sit upon the soul like great black birds

Yet, as mist disappears

With the morning sun

They, too, will flee

With the first faint ray of hope.

CHILD'S PRAYER

Fields of flowers

waving grain

summer sun

and winter rain

all things beautiful to see.

Thank you, God

For all of these.

CARING AND SHARING

Caring and sharing is what life's all about

So the wise men say

And I, though not wise as they,

Agree.

For the days I've cared and shared

Have been my happiest days.

BRAVO

There is so much evil

In the world

Yet so much good

I marvel at it all.

And if I could

I'd give a cheer

For each one who learns to cope

In spite of fear.

Who strives and struggles and learns

And goes on to better things.

Who, when life seems hopeless

Still hopes

For what tomorrow brings.

It is really true

God is so proud of you!

ADVISOR

I find myself quite frequently

Telling God how to run His world.

It isn't that I run my life so well

That I feel like I can give the Universe a whirl.

I grow impatient

With slow moving justice

A thunderbolt here or there

Might hurry things along.

I fret and fuss about the wrongs

Other people do and reading the newspaper

Makes me want to stay in bed.

But, how lost this world would be

If God weren't here

And I were King instead.

So I bow my head

And calmly say,

"They will be done, not mine today."

APPROVAL

God really knew what He was doing

When He made so many different things.

Can you imagine:

The fragrance of lilacs in the spring

Being any more perfect?

Or a maple tree all golden in the fall?

Or a baby's smile, or a redbird's call?

Or a sky full of stars so bright

You ache at the very sight?

Or the first snow on a winter's night?

Or laughing children, black or red,

Yellow, brown or white?

God really knew what He was doing all right!

EASTER

ON PALM SUNDAY

On Palm Sunday

The minister asked the children

What the people said

As Jesus rode into Jerusalem that day

So long ago

And one small boy

With his face aglow

Cried out in a loud voice.

That could be heard a mile

"Hosanna! Hosanna!"

I could almost see God smile!

JESUS

When I was a little girl

I went to Sunday school

and I learned all the pretty stories

about the Baby Jesus.

About Mary, His mother

and being born in a stable

and the bright Star

and the Wise Men who came from far

away, and the Angel who warned Joseph

so wicked King Herod wasn't able

to harm the little Jesus.

Later on,

I learned the not-so-pretty stories

about Jesus, the Man.

About people who didn't understand

His love and plotted to kill Him

and a friend who betrayed Him

and gave Him into the hands

of His enemies. And disciples who ran

at the first sight of trouble

and soldiers who beat Him

and finally drove nails in His feet and hands

and He died on a cross

between two thieves

On a hot afternoon.

And then one fine day

the risen Christ said, "Follow Me,"

and looked my way

and I've been following ever since.

Sometimes gaily, with flags flying

feeling reborn.

And sometimes, reluctantly, lagging

behind, tattered and torn.

And sometimes I've wandered into

Strange roads that turned dark before

I could see my way

and frightened, I've called out to Him

and there He was, waiting for me

to catch up—once more.

So I'm following you, Jesus,

always.

Help me—be my Guide.

Good days or bad days
I'll walk by Your side

to the end.

THE FIRST EASTER

Mary, your son isn't dead

He's alive!

Come quickly, dear one, dry your eyes.

Mary Magdalene, Peter and John say it's true.

And I came as fast

As I could get to you.

I want you to hear for yourself

What they have to say.

Oh, forevermore

Bless this bright and shiny day!

Remember from the night

He was born

All the thoughts you've pondered

In your heart so?

Oh, Mary,

Now you know, now you know.

EASTER MORNING

Oh, Lord,

What a beautiful Easter morning

You have given us.

The weatherman said rain

But here it is,

This shiny bright blue day,

Fragrant with flowers

And the scent of pines

Warm in the sun.

I hear the church bells

In the distance

Pealing out their song of joy

And I sing out, too—

Praise the Lord!

Jesus Christ is risen today!

THE HOCKING VALLEY

THE VALLEY

From my window

Each day I see

The tree-covered hills

That circle my valley.

My valley, I say.

Yet in times gone by,

On another day

Here the Mingoes built their teepees

And an Indian mother

Just like me

Made bread and watched

The children play

The same way I do today.

Her valley, she said

Hers, it was then

Mine, this day

And later on

Some other woman will say,

I love this valley

It belongs to me.

Each rock, each stream

Each cloud, each tree.

And I'll know that feeling

And agree.

THE LOG CABIN

We tramped thru a spring green woods

One day

When the dogwood trees were in bloom.

And there it stood

An old log cabin

A loft and one room.

The door was half opened

So we went inside.

It was only a home

For field mice now

But with what pride

Some man had built

This cabin for his bride.

How long ago

I'll never know

But we saw the biggest oak tree

We've ever seen.

Could he have planted it

As a small slip

Outside his door?

Now it shelters the whole house

And even more.

Or was it old when he came there

And looking at its lofty branches

In the air, say

This is where I'll build my home?

In back were four gnarled apple trees.

We could hear

The hum of bees

And there on the ground

Plain to see

Were the footprints of a deer

That had come to feed.

Under a pile of rocks and twigs

We found their spring.

The water still running sweet and clear.

We saw a small cave

Dug in a hill, near by

A root cellar, it was called

To keep their food, cool and dry.

In my mind

I could see

Children playing

Among the trees.

A young mother

With a gently face

Stirring up a batch

Of Johnny cake.

And I could hear

From the woods in back

The sound of the father's ax.

I could only stand and stare

At all the memories I found there.

It was time to go.

The sun was setting in the sky.

We walked to the clearing's edge

And I turned

And waved goodbye.

WIND & THUNDER—STARS & STORMS

THE WIND

Listen to the wind blow!

Full of furry and blinding snow

Round and round in swirls it goes.

Old house, shelter us from the storm!

As we lie in bed all snug and warm

Listening to the wind blow.

THUNDER

When I was young

I was told

Whenever the thunder

Cracked and rolled

It was the angels bowling.

I'm older and know better now.

But still,

When I hear the thunder

Crack and roll

I seem to hear the angels say

"Come on,

Time to bowl."

A FEELING OF RAIN

There's a feeling of rain

In the air tonight.

The first faint whisper

Of a different breeze

Stirs the leaves on the tree

And is soft against my face.

Moon and stars are in place,

Shining brightly.

Yet there is the scent

Of damp, cool, green woods

Around me,

Soothing as a lullaby.

I hear the night bird's cry

Then suddenly grow still.

When I hold out my hand

I can feel the first raindrops

Fall upon my windowsill.

FIRST STAR AT NIGHT

Star light, star bright

Make a wish

On the first star at night

Food for the hungry

Healing for the sick

Shelter for the homeless

Comfort for the sad

All of this I ask

Little star, little star

I've set you quite a task!

STORM

The rain clouds roll across the sky

Fierce, and mighty and black

The whole world turns dark

Except for jagged flashes

Of lightening

To the south.

The thunder echoes and reechoes

From the hills.

Like an ancient tom-tom.

And I stand looking out the window—

Fascinated.

HOME

HOME IS...

An old white house set high on a hill

Crooked-y floors and worn windowsills

Black shuttered windows and a mailbox that's red

A gold cat named Albert who purrs when he's fed.

Tall maple trees and a front porch swing

A stonewall in back where a cricket sings

A fireplace of brick that my husband built

A four-poster bed and great-grandmother's quilt.

HILL STREET

My street is a friendly street.

It has a special caring spirit

Like a giant heartbeat.

It has a help-each-other feeling,

Bright as a flag unfurled.

Wouldn't it be nice

If all the families of the world

Lived in harmony like my street.

MOVING DAY

It's moving day!

After weeks of careful, than frantic packing

We're on our way.

Now here we are

In our new house.

And we reverse the process

Only this time the work seems less

As the mound of empty boxes

And crumpled newspaper grows.

At last,

I sit in my old rocking chair

To rest my weary bones.

I look around at all

The dear familiar things

And give a happy sigh

We're home.

ANGELS IN MY KITCHEN

On a shelf

In my kitchen

Are three glass angels

Smiling down at me.

No matter where I am

I can turn my head and see

Them shining in the sun

Sparkling in the rain.

Since these gentle figurines

Came to stay

My kitchen hasn't

Seemed the same.

Sometimes I wonder

Can it be

There are three real angels

On the shelf

Smiling down at me?

GENTLE POEMS

DIETER'S PRAYER

Dear God,

Give us this day

Our daily bread

And help us not to eat

Tomorrow's bread

Today.

MEN

Men can be exasperating creatures

Changing every minute.

But what a sad world this would be

With only women in it.

MARY AND MARTHA

God,

Give me Martha's hands

To clean and dust and bake

Bread to share.

But give me a Mary heart

To pray and love

And really care.

THOUGHTS ABOUT A CHIPMUNK

He sits on my stonewall

Small, striped, and brown

Busily eating the food that I bring.

In his wee heart he's thanking me

When it's I who should be thanking him.

FREE TIME

I used to dream

Of hours of free time for

All the extra things I wanted to do

But I never found those free hours.

So I used my odds and ends of time

And all the things I wanted to do

Came true.

THE HERB WOMAN

THE HERB WOMAN

She grew them by her kitchen sill

Basil, Thyme and Chamomile,

Rosemary, Lavender and Dill.

She was old and bent

With twinkly eyes

And loved thru out the countryside

For her medicines made from herbs.

Sage and Mint and Caraway,

Fennel, Chives and Savory.

She lived in an old stone house

That her father built

With his own hands

After he had cleared the land.

It was so fragrant from drying plants

You could smell it a mile away.

People came each day,

To tell her of their ills,

And she gave them packets of her sweet
herbs

And, most often,

They got well.

Tarragon, Anise and Parsley,

Coriander, Bay and Comfrey.

On her death bed

The neighbors gathered round

And said,

"Please don't go-

We need you so."

Gently, she told them,

"Can't you see?

It was God and His herbs,

Not me."

But her friends disagreed.

And when she laid to rest

That sunny winter's day,

Her tombstone read,

The healing circle had to be

God and His herbs and thee.

Sorrel, Rue and Lemon Balm

Tansy, Sesame and Sweet Marjoram.

MELISSA'S HOME

MELISSA'S HOME

They tore down Melissa's house today.

Ninety-two years

It stood on that corner

Surrounded by six tall trees.

Does anyone grieve but me

To see the old house gone

And the velvet lawn

Torn to ribbons by the devouring machine.

Like scavengers the people came

And ripped out mantels, doors and stairs

That Melissa's husband

Had built with loving care

From the walnut trees that used to grow there

But then,

Machines can only tear down the house

But, oh, the memories that still remain

My grandmother used to tell me

Of Melissa's quilting bees and picnics

Under the tree.

And thin sugar cookers with afternoon tea.

And Christmas parties

That filled the whole candle-lit house

I walked on home

Comforted by that thought.

THE ROCKING CHAIR

THE ROCKING CHAIR

I polish it with loving care

My great-great-grandmother's rocking chair.

She gave it to her youngest daughter

On her wedding day.

And there on a quiet farm it stayed

Until the girl who was to be my grandmother

Moved away.

Carefully packed with gentle hands

It traveled to a distant land.

Made of walnut with a satin shine

Now it's mine.

So I polish it with loving care.

My great, great grandmother's rocking chair.

THE STAR QUILT

THE STAR QUILT

By the year 1866,

Young John Hutchinson had come home

From the war,

Cleared some land

And gotten the log house built.

That was the year

His wife, Julie Ann, started to make

Her star quilt.

She used scraps of material,

Like bits of the rainbow,

Gathered from cousins and aunts,

Near and far.

Then carefully cut

Into two hundred and thirty-five

Small eight-sided stars.

When it was time to quilt

Her grandmother came

From three farms down

And Aunt Jessie came from town

To help and gently chide

If the stitches weren't small and neat

And side by side.

Off and on

All winter long

The women worked when chores were thru

And as their busy fingers flew

Grandma told them tales

Of long ago,

When her grandfather first came here

And it was all forestland.

And where Uncle Willy's barn now stands

There was an Indian camp.

So they would talk and sew

Until the sputtering of the lamp

Told them it was time to go.

Julie Ann loved her star quilt

And later on,

Her children loved it, too.

It passed down thru the family

And for ages seemed like new.

It warmed many a small child

And chased away

The winter's chill.

Yet in all her dreams

Never did she guess

That one day her quilt would hang

On the wall of a great museum,

A thing of beauty still,

Tho' faded now and worn.

How proud she'd be

To see this day

And hear all that the people have to say

About her old star quilt

That she made in 1866,

The year John got the log house built.

MR. McCARTY IS DEAD

MR. McCARTY IS DEAD

Mr. McCarty is dead

I feel like crying

But I'll smile instead

Because that's the way

He'd want it.

I loved this dear old man

Who walked with a cane

Past my house each day

And never complained

Of the arthritis that bothered him.

He'd been a farmer

All his life

Until his wife

Died five years ago

And he moved to town

Next door to me.

He taught me how to prune the trees

And entice the bees

To pollinate the flowers

He helped the children find lost balls

And planted tulips for me in the fall.

He had a gentle smile

And quiet faith.

How bright

God's heaven is tonight

With him there.

Mr. McCarty is dead

I feel like crying

But I'll smile instead.

DEE'S PILLOW

Dina A. Meltzer embroidered this pillow for her mother as a Christmas gift. Since our mother didn't give a title to this poem, it is remembered by the family as *Dee's Pillow*. "Marshie" was the nickname her grandchildren's gave to her. This poem speaks so well to who she was and what was really important to her, it is a fitting poem to end this book of her poetry.

DEE'S PILLOW

Please help me

Keep spring in my heart

When days are dark and dreary.

Help me to be as bright

As the summer's sun.

Let my laughter be as gay

As children playing

Under a warm blue sky.

May the fire of love

Burn brightly in my heart

And warm all those I love.

INDEX

This print edition includes all 61 poems from the first hardcover edition published in 1975, plus 80 new poems for this edition, for a total of 141 poems.

For some of her poems, she wrote the month and year it was written. When this date was available, the date has been included after the title in the index. The only indexing concession made was that all poems that started with the word *"The"* were indexed by the following word, thus *The Star Quilt*, is indexed under *Star Quilt, The*. Otherwise, all poems were indexed by their complete title.

A

F

G

R

S

T

W

Y